PRAISES FOR AS A LEADER...

15 POINTS TO CONSIDER FOR MORE INCLUSIVE LEADERSHIP:

"The role of leadership is changing and becoming much more complicated as organizations, supply chains, and public policy makers become more diverse. In his book, Dennis offers some extremely helpful and important principles to consider. What stood out in the 15 points is a reminder that leadership is a lifelong process of learning and adaptation to changing circumstances. It requires the ability to listen to different perspectives, to courageously share difficult feedback, and to make tough decisions when guiding an organization toward a shared vision. This book is easy to read, filled with concrete examples and draws on Dennis' rich personal and professional background! I recommend it to anyone enhancing their skills and effectiveness as an inclusive leader!"

-Effenus Henderson, Chief Diversity Officer, Weyerhaeuser

D1568860

"As a Leader, 15 points to consider for more inclusive leadership is a must read for anyone aspiring to be a more effective leader, no matter what field of concentration, organization, or industry they are in. Author Dennis Brennan draws from his real-life experiences and provides practical advice and insights on how leaders can get results."

-Pat Fong Kushida, President and CEO, California Asian Pacific Chamber of Commerce

"As a Leader, 15 points to consider for more inclusive leadership is like reading what you thought and hoped you knew about leadership and the kind of leader you aspire to be, put into a detailed, step-by-step plan. Dennis does a great job of personalizing his 15 points so you can see yourself in each one. I personally loved the Dennisisms. Each one did make me think!"

-Marilyn Abston Whiting, Director, National Accounts, MTM Recognition

"Told in Dennis' wonderful authentic way, you'll be going back to *As a Leader, 15 points to consider for more inclusive leadership* for direction, guidance and inspiration over the course of your career. This book will stay with you."

-Steve Pemberton, Chief Diversity Officer, Walgreens Author, *A Chance in the World*

AS A LEADER

15

POINTS

TO CONSIDER

FOR MORE

INCLUSIVE

LEADERSHIP

AS A LEADER

15

POINTS
TO CONSIDER
FOR MORE
INCLUSIVE
LEADERSHIP

DENNIS BRENNAN, SPHR

YorkshirePublishing
www.yorkshirepublishing.com
Write Now.

ISBN: 978-1-946977-87-8

As a Leader...15 points to consider for more inclusive leadership

Copyright © 2014 by Dennis Brennan

Yorkshire Publishing
3207 South Norwood Avenue
Tulsa, Oklahoma 74135
www.YorkshirePublishing.com
918.394.2665

For Grandmas Beller & Brennan,
and Mom & Dad.

"All my love, all my life."

Former Global Director, Inclusion
at McDonald's Corporation

CONTENTS

FOREWORD

It was 1996 and I needed a partner, an instigator, someone who knew the system but was bold enough to help drive the changes needed to wake up a sleeping giant. The giant was McDonald's and I had been brought in from the outside to help shake things up. McDonald's had been in a slow decline for many years and the Northern California region was the lowest performer in the country. Back then Human Resources was known as the Personnel Department and their priorities were payroll and benefits. I needed a people leader, a change agent – someone who could help me evaluate talent, develop them, place them in the best seat, and get them to believe in themselves. Dennis Brennan was that instigator, and he became my Director of Human Resources.

I have had the opportunity to run businesses around the world and see many different leaders in action. A constant topic of discussion in our leadership meetings is people talent, and the challenge of getting people to see their own capabilities and unleashing them. I look for leaders who can work with different thinkers and exceed expectations in business results and people development. This is what I call inclusive leadership. It's about having individuals feel ownership in the mission and taking responsibility for their personal growth.

In reading *As a Leader, 15 points to consider for more inclusive leadership*, I found valuable lessons. In my experience with Dennis, he modeled these points as he helped lead our Regional Staff to higher levels of performance. This included him reaching out to the community to make business connections to enhance the brand; and he was able to bring many different groups and people together and get results. The 15 points found in this book can enlighten any leader in bringing out the best in their people; and with his Dennisisms, I can see the serious fun Dennis relates in people leadership – "Change people or change people" is what it's all about.

Oh, and the results back in 1996 – within one year, all with talent that was already based there, our business unit went from thirty-nine out of thirty-nine to second in the country; and that was followed by consecutive first in the country the next two years. This with basically the same people, except for a few bad apples who had to be moved out – or as Dennis would say "changed" – as they were talent blockers in the people formation.

Dennis Brennan was my instigator; he became the first Director of Inclusion for McDonald's Corporation. He gets people to see things and think differently. His book is an excellent guide of how leaders can help teams and individuals reach their maximum potential. As you read this book, I am confident you will find more than one thing you can use to become a more inclusive leader. I encourage you to leverage the examples and lessons Dennis has shared.

-Raul Alvarez
Chairman of the Board, Skylark Co., Ltd.
Board of Directors: Dunkin' Brands, Eli Lilly and Company, Lowe's Company, Inc., Realogy Holding
Past President & COO, McDonald's Corporation

EVERYTHING STARTS SOMEWHERE

Learn from every situation.
Show—don't tell.
Encourage—don't discourage.
Act positive,
Be positive,
Think positive.
Be successful!

Words I've tried to live by since writing them down in the mid 1980s.

Leadership comes in many forms, but I'm confident in saying that we are all leaders in some instance, manner, or style. Others look to us for answers to questions or situations—some very simple, some more complex. We interact with others and provide perspective. We are leaders.

However, in the context of today's society, leaders appear to be more elevated. They lead families, teams, committees, companies, institutions, movements, religions, political parties, nations, and so many more areas that it would be exhaustive to define all the ways people lead. Leaders are elected, appointed, or asked to serve by others. Someone else finds something of value in what they offer. They lead others in actions, thoughts, results. There is a saying that goes "Managers get things done; leaders get things done…through other people." It is how leaders get these things done, or other things leaders should consider, that will be the focus of my book.

My first recognized leaders were my mother and father. They taught me things, obviously from birth, in the only way they knew how, from their experiences. I looked up to them; I imitated them in their actions and words. Not once did I see them go to a leader's manual or a "How to Raise a Child" handbook. They treated me as they had been treated, but as I learned much later in life, it was better than they were treated during their younger years. There may have been omissions; they may have taken risks, but overall, as leaders of the family, they did the best they could with all the knowledge, experience, and insight they gained and had at their disposal. As the oldest of four children, all of whom have graduated college, are healthy, and have satisfactory careers in our chosen fields, I can say with confidence that my parents did a darn good job *leading* our family.

As a leader, no matter how you define it, people look up to you for some reason. You don't have to say one word, yet your actions will speak volumes about your confidence, your knowledge, and your willingness to help and assist someone else or groups of people to higher levels of knowledge, achievement, or satisfaction. Cultural norms, whatever they may be, define you as a leader. What works for a leader in one culture may not work the same for that leader in another culture, and culture is defined in many, many different ways, and sometimes we have no idea what the cultural norm is even when we are right in the middle of it.

I have strived to fit in most of my life. I was a very active child who was a remedial reader in my elementary school days, an underachiever in my middle and high school days, and then an above average student and national caliber athlete in my college days. In my professional career, I became a confident advisor, facilitator, and speaker on small and large stages in the United States and a number of foreign countries. I have challenged myself to impress others so I could fit in and feel good about myself and my achievements. I have been a recognized leader in many different situations, for many different reasons, with some very interesting results, considering my past. I was president of my junior class in college. I tried out and almost made the Washington Redskins football team. I read aloud Dr. Seuss's book *Oh, the Places You'll Go!* in an Irish brogue to fifty-two national outstanding assistant school principals. I was granted a US patent for a Crutch Beverage holder, and I was elected *twice* as chairman of the board of a large metropolitan Urban League. It is from these and many other experiences and perspectives that my life's mission had its genesis in the early 1970s but wasn't defined until the late 1980s—*to help people do things they don't think they can do.* We are all leaders based on our life experiences, and we can help others achieve what they don't think they can. We must be open to learning. We must be open to sharing, and I've learned we must be open to taking risks.

"Our minds live in the past, in the present, adapting to the future"—a phrase I came up with to relate how our past experiences are used on a daily basis as we look to tomorrow and the unknown. We must include as much as we can from our past and present, those things we find enjoyable and maybe even those things we don't like or don't understand, to be a leader for tomorrow. My mother always said to learn something new every day. I wish I had paid more attention to my very smart mother when I was younger, but alas, I was too distracted by my present to think about my future.

This book is written with the intent to help people do things they don't think they can do. It is for all those people who need someone to believe in them, to help them grow, and to help them achieve what they can only imagine. It was inspired by my parents, Don and Pat (deceased) Brennan, and my college football and track coach Rollie Greeno (deceased) who all believed in me when I didn't fully believe in myself. They collectively showed me and pushed (sometimes shoved) me to excellence that I never imagined. Through it all, my wife Trudy has been my compass, grounding me in the fundamentals of faith and "holding down the fort" as I was off on my professional career path. She is the foundation of our home, and for our two ladies, Jamie and Heather, who have taught me more than they will ever know about not only being a father but also about a much younger and more diverse perspective as two women in today's society.

I dedicate this book to all those people that throughout my life, for the good and the bad lessons, have taught me how to believe in the person I see in the mirror. I pray you find some nuggets of value in what you are about to read so you can become a more effective, more inspirational, more inclusive leader. Enjoy the read!

POINT 1—
ORGANIZATIONAL CULTURE
AS A LEADER...

> Point 1: Don't assume you know the organization culture, even if people tell you you do or you've been there forever. You have to be a continual student of the business and understand from where the organization has come—the good, the bad, and the ugly—and where it is going. There is always more to learn.

As a premise, *every* organization has a culture. Understanding it, adapting to it, and succeeding in it are the challenges faced by anyone entering into this new culture. You are actually attempting to merge your *personal* culture with a *professional* culture and have them appear seamless. You are trying to fit in and achieve some level of success that is defined differently but hopefully in symmetry on both the personal and professional levels.

So what is "culture"? One definition from the Merriam-Webster dictionary:

> Culture (noun)—(an) integrated pattern of human knowledge, belief, and behaviour that is both a result of and integral to the human capacity for learning and transmitting knowledge to succeeding generations. Culture thus consists of language, ideas, beliefs,

customs, taboos, codes, institutions, tools, techniques, works of art, rituals, ceremonies, and symbols. It has played a crucial role in human evolution, allowing human beings to adapt the environment to their own purposes rather than depend solely on natural selection to achieve adaptive success. Every human society has its own particular culture, or sociocultural system. Variation among cultures is attributable to such factors as differing physical habitats and resources; the range of possibilities inherent in areas such as language, ritual, and social organization; and historical phenomena such as the development of links with other cultures. An individual's attitudes, values, ideals, and beliefs are greatly influenced by the culture (or cultures) in which he or she lives. Culture change takes place as a result of ecological, socioeconomic, political, religious, or other fundamental factors affecting a society.

Wow, that is one heck of a definition! It is, or strives to be, all encompassing. In the context of this book, since it is focused primarily on leadership, as in leading self and others, I would like to use the element of "human society" as the modifier for any type of organization and thus the culture within.

Let's break organization culture into a few categories so you might see how you fit into an organization to gain an understanding of its culture.

NEW TO AN ORGANIZATION:

When you are new to an organization, your view of the organization is more from the public view or maybe from friends or relatives that work at the organization. You have an "outsider looking in" viewpoint. One thing to understand from this outsider viewpoint, what you read or hear about an organization is from someone else's perspective. You must form your own perspective, your own opinion, on what the organizational culture is and how you must adapt to it. Note I say *you* must adapt to it, not the other way around.

Every organization has a culture, no matter how big or small. It can come from the founder or the owner, the current CEO or executive director, the new chancellor or provost, or even a new Pope. Whoever is at the top, the organizational culture is an evolutionary reflection of this person. They set the tone, the pace, and the interactions. When you join an organization, you are assimilating into *its* culture. You continually assess the culture of the organization against your personal culture for alignment in your leadership role. Nothing is perfect and don't expect there to be perfect alignment, but if the vast majority of elements align, you will continue to progress with your assimilation.

We have all seen, read out, or even used the good ol' 90 or 100 day plan for a new position. When being considered for a new position, we sometimes formulate this theoretical plan to impress those who will be making the decision on the position. The paradox of this plan is that it's a theory, it's a guess.

You don't have the fact of future experience to put into your proposed game plan. Based on *your* current experience and some anecdotal research, you have come up with a theoretical plan to impress others on what you *might* do with your limited knowledge of the expectations of the position. The practicality of your plan can only be proven over time, and far too many leaders abandon their proposed plan when the realities of their new position reveal themselves during what I call the 3-3-6 of their new position.

The 3-3-6 is a simple theory of assimilation I developed over the years when you take on a new job or a new leadership role. For the first three months in your new position, you struggle with knowing the people, the places, and even some of the "things" of your new responsibilities. You feel somewhat lost, a bit confused, and you may wonder if you made the right decision to take the position.

In your second three months, you are becoming more confident with connecting the dots on the people, the places, and the "things" of your new responsibilities. You are learning about the culture and how things work, whom they work with, and what work is expected.

During your next six months, you are pretty much on a roll. You are mastering the people, places, and things of your position. People are getting to know you and your capacities, and you are forming opinions and perspectives with all whom you interact.

That's your first year! I have seen far too many leaders become frustrated during the early days, weeks, or months of their new position simply because they don't comprehend the need to assimilate and learn the culture. They jump in trying to change the world to demonstrate their knowledge, skills, and abilities without taking into account the organization culture. Due to their early innocent ignorance, they may disrespect peer or senior leadership with their aggressiveness; they are not aware of the silent leaders within their group because they simply don't know who they are. In their pursuit of excellence, they try to fit in by thrusting their experiences and their values into the organization because that is what they have seen work in the past for other leaders. They end up turning more people off to their abilities rather than demonstrating their leadership potential.

It is during the early stages of your career that patience and persistence pay off. Stay on plan, but be willing to adapt.

BEEN WITH AN ORGANIZATION FOR LESS THAN TEN YEARS

As you approach ten years with an organization, it is a testament to your perseverance that you are learning to adapt within the organization as a leader. You are getting results, you know how to maneuver within the organization on matters of importance, and you are proving your worth and the investment the organization has made in you.

The key here is to not become complacent. Continue to learn from those around you while acknowledging the heritage of the organization and looking to the future for growth opportunities personally and professionally. As you look for growth opportunities, look both inside the organization and outside the organization. What is your competition doing to keep ahead of the curve? Who is your competition networking with? Who are they speaking with? What trials are they putting themselves through to test their mettle?

Now you may note I do not define "competition" in the above paragraph. You may assume that I am referring to external organizations that compete within your industry, and that is partially correct. However, I'm also referring to those *individuals* you are in competition with professionally for opportunities that may raise your value to your organization. It is during this still relatively early stage of your career that finding advisors or mentors who can assist with creating your future success will be of value. You cannot and nor should you attempt your career path by yourself. Seek out those who have already been down your chosen path for guidance and insight on how to proceed with more efficiency and effectiveness. If you don't ask for help, you'll never get it.

A caution here is warranted: Don't hook your wagon to just one advisor. In your personal life, count how many advisors you have for all the various aspects of your life such as doctors, where to shop, where to get your hair done, bankers, and so forth. I am *very* confident you do not have just one advisor for all your personal life activities. Why then would you have only one advisor for your professional career activities? Now I'm not saying you should have a gallery of advisors, but I would offer that a group of three to five advisors from the functions or experiences you aspire to would be manageable to evolve your leadership skills. As with the changes in your personal life that require changing of advisors, so too is the requirement to keep your current advisor group relevant to how your career evolves. If done well, former advisors transition to advocates for you well into the future and you may never know what they have done for you.

BEEN WITH AN ORGANIZATION FOR MORE THAN TEN YEARS

It is becoming rarer in today's work places to find those individuals with ten and more years in an organization. We are, if not already, fast becoming a world of accelerated demands and satisfaction. "If I can't find job satisfaction here, I'll go somewhere else." Ever heard that from a subordinate? Ever felt that way personally? As a leader, of yourself and others, nothing is static. You must be continually learning to remain relevant in today's organizational environment.

The global workforce continues to blur the edges of distinction and offer exceedingly more diverse candidates for every position available. As a leader, how are you leveraging this new workforce to the advantage of yourself and your organization? What are you learning about the people that are different from you? After all, don't you like to work and shop where you see yourself reflected? Don't you like to work where the mission and values of the organization reflect those of your own? Nothing is as it was in the past, and today will not be like it is in the future. The Marine Corps has a saying, "Improvise, adapt, overcome." As a leader in today's competitive environment, this credo can serve you well as you learn what you don't know; adapt it to your current and near future challenges; overcome those seen and unseen obstacles that will inevitably be thrown in your path and leverage the organizational culture to your advantage.

An effective leader is one who is not satisfied with themselves or where they want to move others. Effective leaders continually challenge their own learning and understanding by wanting to learn more, and the learning may not be in their direct line of sight. Learning about topics or functions or even different people that *may* have an effect on your position or your function allows you to gain insight into possible leverage or avoidance points that can affect your results. Don't be afraid to step out into uncomfortable areas. When you take that risk, you may gain knowledge that will surprise you and may impress others by your example. You also gain confidence that will embolden you to take even larger risks that may yield higher results as you continue to grow.

POINT 2—ACCOUNTABILITY
AS A LEADER...

> Point 2: Understand that you are accountable for getting things done without being told what to do or how to do it. "We are only interested in results."

"Just get it done!" As a leader, have you ever heard that phrase? As a leader, have you ever said that phrase? Harry Truman, the thirty-third president of the United States, had a famous saying sitting on his desk in the White House, "The buck stops here!" meaning it all stops at him; he's the president, the person in charge, the one accountable. As a leader, you can't pass the buck. You must make decisions; you must get results. It is in the "how you do it" that all your leadership magic happens.

Let's start by considering what accountable can mean. In a leadership context, it usually means the person responsible for decisions and actions, as in "you are accountable for," "I'll hold you accountable for," or "The results are on your head." However, can *one* person do everything so that they can rightly *be* held accountable for all the actions going into getting the desired result? The easy answer to this question is a simple no. However, the more complicated answer to the question is yes—one person can be held responsible for getting results because they are the leader. The leader sets the direction and accepts the recommendations of those who report to them, or they reject the recommendations based on information they have acquired and they ask for alternatives. The leader is accountable.

"I don't care how you get it done, just get it done!" I cringe when I hear this statement coming from a person in authority. It is a very poor demonstration of leadership, especially if someone were to take the statement literally. As a leader, you have obligations that go far beyond your job description. There are legal obligations of all kinds; there may be statutory or regulatory obligations based on your position. There may be country or national ethical and moral obligations to consider. All this places a pretty heavy burden of responsibility on the leader accountable for getting results. The daily news streams have a plethora of leadership transitions for those who could not get the expected results or did not meet the expected standard or didn't act in an ethical manner. However, there are vastly more success stories than you can imagine that go unheralded. Successful leadership happens every day, and leaders do get results the right way far more often than not.

Sit back, and let your mind drift to the leadership person or two that you admire. I won't ask you to close your eyes because then you couldn't read what comes next. What are the single-word or short-phrase attributes you think about when you mentally think of this person? I might offer…inspirational, knowledgeable, connected, hard-charger, uncompromising, motivational, good listener, detailed, high expectations, demanding, patient, good teacher, confident, or sincere. Add your attributes to the list. As a leader, do you display the attributes you admire in others so others can admire them in you? Do you even know how others see you as a leader?

As a leader, you are many things to many people, but most of all, you demonstrate your standards for all to see, even when no one is looking. As a leader, you are always on stage because people listen to what you say, how you say it, when you say it, and even sometimes when you don't say anything. You are the leader, you are in charge, you must know what needs to be done, and you must know how to do it—lead us to the results we need. Oh, if it were that simple. And when *you* don't get the expected results, isn't it amazing how quickly your support begins to fall away?

It's not all doom and gloom. As you came up during your professional career, you were acquiring skills and abilities that at the time you didn't think would mean much. After all, when I was in typing class in high school, little could I have imagined the very basic expectation of today to use my typing skills on a keyboard in the variety of ways I do or the simple and advanced elements of mathematics to calculate financial projections or analyze trends or accurately reflect the fiscal health of my family or my business. When I studied civics and historic leaders, did I understand that impressions were being made in my mind that would be of value in future leadership roles I could have never dreamed? Sometimes yes, but often the answer was no. Thankfully, impressions were being made, impressions that have proven valuable as I have evolved in my personal and professional life. You have similar impressions that have served you well and can serve you better as you grow in your positions.

As a leader, there are spoken and unspoken expectations of you to add value to an organization. You are expected to get results, ethically, morally, and, I will add, inspirationally. You can't be told everything as in how, when, or even why you should do something. It is up to you to identify the need, gather the expertise that *may* be needed, and move toward or exceed the expected result. You must rely on yourself, your knowledge, and the knowledge and experience of those you gather to achieve your objectives and your results. Never misunderstand that as a leader, it is up to you to make the decisions needed to achieve the lasting results that are expected of you for the health and well-being of your organization and, more importantly, for you as the leader.

You are the one in charge; you are the one accountable. Use the resources—people, time, and money—at your disposal to achieve the results for which you are accountable.

POINT 3—
ORGANIZATION DIRECTION
AS A LEADER...

> Point 3: You must demonstrate the direction the
> organization is going in, but not necessarily the path
> that should be taken.

You are the leader. People look up to you because of your
position. You have been granted authority for some reason.
You are supposed to know what to do, where to go, and how
to get there, right? You are the all-knowing, all-seeing leader.
You can predict the future and make it come to pass, right?
After all, as the leader, *you* know everything. Oh, if it were
that simple.

As a leader in an organization, there is a certain expectation of knowledge that comes with your position. There is
also access to greater knowledge that comes with successively
higher position levels as you move up the ladder that can be
leveraged in many ways. The more you learn and know, the
more you can apply your learning in an influential manner,
the more you can affect the course of direction you set to
achieve the expected results of your superiors, and please
understand that everyone has a superior or boss.

How does this person see you setting the direction for
your subordinates? Is it the direction that your superior

expects? How do you know? It is by your demonstration, your actions, and your interactions that your superior continues to support you along your leadership path. As long as you are moving in generally the same direction as your superior leadership, things will progress well. If you start to stray from the expected path, a good leader will reach out for clarity, for alignment on expectations or confirmation that the wider path you are taking, even though it might be stretching previously traveled paths, may still lead to the expected results, or to even better, higher results.

So what does this "demonstration of leadership" look like? How will I know it when I see it? Let's first start by describing what it is not.

Think of those times when you have seen or heard a leadership peer speak on the topic of where the organization is going; someone below the C-suite. Ever scratched your head and think, "Where in the heck did they come up with that perspective?" People hear things differently from the same source all the time. We each have different life experiences that cause us to put a different meaning on the same thing. Sometimes people add their own color commentary to erroneously emphasize a point; sometimes they try to impress their audience. The trap these ego leaders fall into is they can't remember what they said, to whom, or in what context their comment was made. These leaders are inconsistent at best. They may have streaks of brilliance, but their star burns out quickly because they confuse more people then they inform.

They cannot demonstrate consistent leadership, which is detrimental to any organization.

All leaders, hopefully, want to add value, want to add their own unique experience perspective to the success of a company. After all, we all want to be better off tomorrow than we are today, right? A leader must demonstrate through their actions and their words that they understand where an organization is going, why the organization is going there, how things will be better off along the designated path, and, most importantly, how customers, clients, and employees will benefit from this direction and the landmarks as everyone travels this path together. They must stay within the guidelines of an organization's directional message, or they risk being detoured off course by their own lack of alignment.

As your audience listens to your messaging, the ol' "what's in it for me" axiom begins to play in their minds. Your audience, whomever they may be, is listening from the perspective of a subordinate looking at the leader who knows where we are going, why we need to go there, and why this is the right path. If they don't *see* you acting supportive, don't *hear* you speaking supportive, don't *see* and *hear* positive results and comments, then who and what are they to believe? If they can't see a benefit for themselves in your message and actions, then they will begin to disengage from a contribution standpoint and begin looking for something or someone who can offer more of a confirming direction so they can see some higher benefit for their contributions. After all, as my leader,

I am following your direction, and I need to feel confident in the direction I hear from you and see from you.

The more informed you are as a leader, the more confident your decisions will be. The more confident your decisions are along the general direction of the organization, the more alignment occurs between your group and other groups within the organization. The more alignment there is along this organizational direction, the more efficient and effective the organization can be. The more efficient and effective an organization is, their potential for return on investment is increased, the better their business and employment image will be, and the better organization leadership, as a whole, will be viewed from inside and outside the organization.

Leaders lead people in the direction they believe is right. People follow a leader because of their belief in that leader. Where an organization is going and when it will get there is the responsibility of leadership to determine. *How* an organization will get there is left up to the collective expertise of all within an organization. Effective leaders have the ability to tease expertise and insight out of their subordinates to continue moving along the directional path. Effective leaders also learn along the way as they don't know everything, which may be a surprise to some people, but it is true.

Successful leaders easily state they will learn from their subordinates while guiding them along the path of success. They will achieve success together. The leader will provide the context, the environment, and the encouragement for their group of individuals to move beyond where any one person may be able to go. They will move forward together.

I have been known to say to those who have worked for me, early in our relationship, that I will not answer your questions. This has always been met with strong question marks on the faces of my team members. I then make a quick commitment to each of them—"I will guide you to the answer(s)." I have found that by not providing direct, easy answers to subordinate questions, it requires them to seek answers on their own. However, I have always been open to discuss their findings or provide further guidance. This is an early lesson I was taught by my mother.

"Mom, how do you spell _____?"

"Sound it out and go look it up in the dictionary" would be her response.

"Mom, what does _____ mean?"

"Go look it up in the dictionary."

After awhile I quit asking Mom those questions because I knew what her response would be, and I just went to the dictionary and found the answer myself. I began to use the resources available to me and actually found it to be much quicker. An added benefit is that I became more self-reliant and learned I appeared more self-confident.

By guiding people to answers, not only are you reinforcing your knowledge on the topic, but you are also demonstrating how others can use the resources at their disposal, sometimes unknown, to seek out answers for themselves. This incrementally builds their knowledge base and confidence. Though this method does take more upfront time in some instances, in the long run it has proven to save you time as you will be answering less questions and seeing more independence and results from your team. You might also hear about external observations and comments regarding your team being more independent and confident, which builds the positive perception of your leadership competence in building talent and influencing others.

POINT 4—
NOT JUST YOUR WAY
AS A LEADER...

> Point 4: Understand that your way is not always the best way. Learn from others and allow some of their ideas to come forward, even if it may not be exactly how you would have done it. It builds confidence in those you work with and relationships that will have value sometime in the future.

In my very first human resources manager position at a distribution center in Landover, Maryland, way back in 1979, I had a very competent secretary. At the time, I was an executive trainee with a large retail organization, and this was my first large position beyond that of a retail store department manager. The distribution center had almost four hundred employees from nonunion warehouse employees to an organized delivery service, to three satellite appliance service centers, and a large truck tire service operation. We had a lot going on, and I set the people direction, made the decisions, and told people what to do. I was the boss, and I knew what was expected of me. I knew the what, when, and how for everything, or so I thought. One day, I asked Linda, my secretary, to do something the way I described above. She stood there for a moment and then asked if she could say something.

One thing that I very much appreciated about Linda was that she was very efficient. She got things done with very few errors, which was extremely important when you consider she was primarily responsible for the payroll processing of about four hundred people. Back in those days, it was all done by hand and an adding machine. So thinking that her question would be to clarify something, I said sure. What came forth was a life lesson that I remember to this day.

"Dennis, I don't have a problem with you telling me what to do. I don't have a problem with you telling me when you need it done, but I do have a problem with you telling me *how* to do it. Let me use what I have between my ears to get it done when you want it! If it's not done right, I know you will let me know." I sat there for what seemed like a long time and just looked at her. She just looked back. I finally mustered the guts to say okay. I then followed that up with an apology as I did not realize I was diminishing her abilities with my leadership style. From that day on, we had a more respectful relationship. We taught each other respect, or should I say, Linda taught me to respect her and her abilities as an individual. We became a very good team, and I have taken that lesson forward in all the positions I have held since that learning.

Do you listen when a direct report has the guts to tell you something? Can you see yourself as others see you, seeing you? It is hard to be vulnerable and be willing to learn from others when you are supposed to be the one in charge, the one in the know. However, the lessons that you learn can be life changing.

The exchange with Linda continued to have an effect on my leadership perspective as my career advanced. I did not presume to know everything. Oh, I read and studied and dialoged to confirm understanding with my boss, but I did not presume to have all the answers when my direct reports came to me with questions about specific topics. I learned to ask questions for confirmation and to listen. What did *they* know? What could *they* do? What was *their* opinion? What direction did *they* think we should go? I learned to ask more questions than just provide an answer. It is from my lesson with Linda that my statement of "I will not answer your question, but I will guide you to the answer" came. Over the years, this "question back" approach has served me well in the positions I've been privileged to hold. In every position I have held since my 1979 lesson, I have continued to empower those people that have worked for me, and it has benefited us all. It has also truly paid dividends far beyond what I know in what past subordinates have related to me as they have moved along with their career.

How 'bout you? What are you doing to let the knowledge growing within those you lead come forth to benefit you and your organization? How are you going to demonstrate you are open to inquiry on solutions you can't imagine? It is challenging to ask the question and then only listen to the reply. However, by listening to what those who report to you have to say, you can gain more than you might imagine.

POINT 5—BE INQUISITIVE
AS A LEADER...

> Point 5: Be inquisitive. Don't be afraid to say, "Help me understand" or "Can you explain how that links to our business drivers or our values or…"

Departed author Stephen Covey continues to be an inspiration to many leaders even today. In the mid-1980s I read his book *Seven Habits of Highly Effective People* and was inspired in many ways. I later became a facilitator of the Seven Habits course to help others realize how they could be more effective utilizing the principles in Dr. Covey's book. Highly Effective People Habit 5 is "Seek first to understand, then be understood." Seek first to understand. Ask questions, listen, ask more questions, seek first to understand; then you will have the opportunity to express your position, your perspective, your opinion, but "seek first to understand."

Far too many leaders, at various levels, are of the opinion because of their position that they know it all. "What can others, especially those that report to me, teach me that I don't already know? After all, I was put in this position because of my knowledge, my skills, and my ability to get results."

I would offer that it is the wise and humble leader that *doesn't* believe they know it all; that there is much more to learn, more insight to gain, and they can learn from almost anyone, anywhere, at any time, even when they least expect it.

A strong leader actively seeks out information from a variety of sources to increase and enhance their perspective on various issues, challenges, and simple, basic information. They look for opposing views to their position so they have some measure of confidence that they are looking at their position from a 360-degree perspective to take in as many viewpoints as possible. This helps to ensure their chosen path is the confident path to pursue.

Think for a moment about a time when you were sitting in a meeting and offered your opinion, asked or not on a matter, and someone speaks up and says, "I don't agree with you!" What is your first reaction? What is the first thing you do in response? For most people, it is one of defense; you start to defend your position or perspective. You justify yourself by expanding on the information you have just related. You attempt to reexplain what you just said all the while giving credence to your challenger and possibly putting questions in the minds of the other meeting attendees as to how you came to your position.

What if you did not react to the challenge? What if you absorbed the statement and thought about it for only a quick moment? What might you really want to do? What might be a more inclusive response to learn more? I would offer that you would wonder why the person just made that statement. What basis is there for the disagreement? What information might the person have that you are not aware of? What you really have at this pivotal moment is a void of information.

You simply don't know why the person made the statement. You must find out why they made their statement to reach higher, more collaborative ground.

A better approach to a verbal challenge is one of inquiry, a question or two to seek understanding. "Help me understand why you disagree with my position." Help *me* understand. By not reacting to your challenger with a defensive response and their possible need for some sort of recognition, you put them in the spotlight to defend their remark. You then have the opportunity to dialogue about, rather than defend, your position.

Usually, misunderstandings occur when parties refuse to seek a deeper understanding and they react at an emotional level, define the matter at hand based on their life experiences, and don't think to dialogue about an issue. Dialogue takes effort; it takes time, and people today are busy. They are focused on their perspective without thinking about other perspectives that may bring about a different, possibly better outcome. By investing some effort and time in a constructive dialogue of understanding, your information return will likely be of more value.

When dialogue occurs, when clarifying questions are asked, when more thoughts are brought to the table, richer ideas and solutions are brought forth. People really do see things differently, and it is the talented and insightful leader that has the skills to ask the deep questions and leverage the difference around them that will bring the best out of individuals, teams, and themselves.

POINT 6—BE NIMBLE
AS A LEADER...

> Point 6: Understand you work in an extremely fast-paced time, which requires you to be nimble, but you must conduct due diligence, in all that is done worldwide, which may appear to be slow.

Instant messaging. Instagram. Google Instant. E-mail. Skype. Facetime. Bing. Yahoo. YouTube. Facebook. Twitter. Foursquare. Streaming. Google Glass. In touch now; ability to reach one, hundreds, thousands, millions in an instant. Letting people know what you need, what you have, what you are doing, where you are doing it, and even how you are doing it…all at the touch of a key. My, how communicating has changed, and changed so quickly, and continues to change even as you read this book. If you don't know something within ten seconds, you're slow, you're out of touch, and you're behind. People are learning more at an earlier age and at a faster pace than their more tenured, more experienced peers and leaders. Wow, and as a leader, you have to keep up or you fall behind!

In the ever-changing, more rapidly changing global world of business learning and communications, can you as a leader stay abreast of all that is happening to ensure you are doing your best? The accelerated and exponential increase in technology requires individuals and leaders to adapt on a daily basis to the environment around them in order to not fall behind your competition, your peers, or even your subordinates.

I say you must be nimble. No one, not even IBM's super-computer Watson, knows *everything*. To play off the Watson theme, you must continually program yourself with information that is important to you and your mission in order to remain competent, competitive, and relevant in your leadership role. You must be acquiring information in collaboration with others. However, information gathered today, from unconfirmed or unreliable sources, can lead to dramatic errors in communication and decisions, which will be attributed to the leader communicating the message and, potentially, the quick demise of said leader.

Checking, double-checking, and even triple-checking facts and sources have saved many a person from poor decisions. I recall a newspaper editor's edict that all facts must be verified from three independent sources. That is a great rule of thumb, but in today's fast-paced times, that would be terribly slow. However, the diligence illustrated by the edict is a reminder to leaders that even if you are pressed to make decisions, conduct a discovery of due diligence to remove as much question and doubt as possible.

Another rule I have followed, one from retired army general, former chairman of the joint chiefs of staff, and former secretary of state Colin Powell, "Don't wait until you have enough facts to be 100 percent sure." General Powell goes on to say you must "go with your gut when you are in the 70 to

80 percent range. Waiting for a 100 percent confirmation will undeniably put you behind those who have gone with their gut and passed you by."

A third rule of thumb I follow, my third confirmation, is to "go slow to go fast," a quote that is attributed to many but one that makes so much sense. "Go slow"—gather as much relevant information as possible along the way. "To go fast"—so you can continue competitively along your path of success. I have been known to rephrase this as being "strategically slow"—holding back because of a gut instinct, a sixth sense, something that is hard to explain to someone else, but a sense that there is more diligence that can be done before I move to the go forward decision of the strategic objective.

The "strategic objective," or as I have been known to say, the "big picture" objective, the end destination, the place I'll know it when I see it. But how will I know it when I see it? Ah, the big question. I will offer the following:

- *If* you are nimble enough to engage all those around you for their differing opinions,

- *If* you *listen* to what is being offered without making initial judgments,

- *If* you can discern the variations in the recommendations yet still see their context in the big picture,

- *If* you can sense the value in the pieces of information that by themselves do not appear to hold much value,

- *Then* you will be able to craft a unique mosaic from your due diligence pieces that creates a big picture reality that everyone will be able to see.

It is patience, and it is diligence. It requires discipline, dedication, and insight. It is art. It is your own future picture that you have put together from your research and your discovery. It is one that you crafted with your due diligence. However, I would offer it is a picture of confidence that will stand up to the speed of our times.

POINT 7—
STRATEGIC PLANNING
AS A LEADER...

Point 7: Understand the lead-time element of strategic planning. It's not always clear at the beginning, but the organization is very good at having an idea of where they want to go, but not necessarily how or the most efficient way to get there. That's where you can help!

"Would you tell me, please, which way I ought to go from here?"

"That depends a good deal on where you want to get to."

"I don't much care where…"

"Then it doesn't matter which way you go."

This paraphrase of a directional exchange from the book *Alice in Wonderland* by Lewis Carroll, between Alice and the Cheshire Cat sitting up in a tree at a fork in the road has been used over and over in strategic planning workshops I have attended over the years. "If you don't know where you're going, than any path will do." A competent leader must have an idea of the general direction they should be going, especially if they are responsible for any kind of organization. Without direction, you are lost, personally and professionally.

Strategic planning, the concept of thinking about and planning your direction, allows a leader to conceptualize the general direction they feel they should go. This is different from the tactical aspect of thinking and planning that goes into more granular detail on the direction. During my career, I've learned a four-step process for this type of planning that I have found to be of great value: (1) strategic thinking, (2) strategic planning, (3) tactical thinking, (4) tactical planning. Notice you think before you plan. You must give thought and have ideas before you can do something with them, but you must first be strategic, you must stay out of the weeds, and you must not go to action steps until you know where you want to go.

"But can't we just get to solutions?" The short answer to this short-sighted question is yes, but are you creating solutions to the correct issues? "Creating solutions to the correct issues" is the question best answered by strategic thinking and planning.

Strategic thinking—the time to sit and think; time to think about and discuss; time to discuss what ifs and what abouts; time to dialogue about the buts, ifs, and I wishes; and time to discuss the future. You are crafting a time and place in the future. You are describing what your future will look, feel, and be like. You are on the edge of dreaming, but you are still in reality. You are thinking about making the impossible possible. You have no restrictions, no barriers. You do have wonders as to how or who or what or when as you strategically think. However, you are only concerned with that far out "if we could" place that will be a likely destination.

Strategic planning—Do you have the resources to go where you want to go? Are you organized the way you should be to achieve your strategic vision? What are those things that work in your favor, and what are those things that will work against you or get in your way? Who are your advocates, and who are your dissenters? How do you know? As you begin to develop the strategic layout, the strategic plan or path that will arrive at your thinking destination, you must constantly challenge yourself to *not* get into the details of the how you will achieve the plan, not yet. Stay in the dream picture, that "if we could do _____" or "people will be saying _____ when we _____."

If strategic thinking is your destination, then strategic planning begins to define your geography, or where you will be realizing your dream. You are sketching your path, defining your trail, but you are not yet doing the paving or marking the road or installing road signs. You are cutting your way through the woods to establish the trail.

When you get a little lost or question your path, use the concept of think, plan, do, and act. I have found these four steps align very well with the four steps of thinking and planning I related above. Keep these four simple steps in mind when you start to get off track. These will help you stay on task during your planning process. Think: See where you want to go. Plan: Have a sense of how you will get there. Do:

Define the resources you will use to move. Act: Who will be doing what? Another catchy phrase comes to mind—"Plan your work, and then work your plan."

When you have laid out the strategic plan, the general high level of "from here to there," it is then time to begin your tactical thinking work. It is in this segment you define the work to be done, or the Do. However, again, stay high level, but be more defined than in your strategic planning element. You are getting more specific with the work to be done considering your resources, your organization, your allies, and your opposers. You are *thinking* through the ifs, ands, and buts of your plan. You are better detailing high level actions at the various organization levels and then running them through your success scenarios to define omissions. After all, it is better to surface your consideration omissions early in trial scenarios than farther down the line in real situations. Your cost is *much* less, and your chance of success increases with every solution defined early rather than later. Spend more upfront time during this stage even if it appears lengthy. It really will save you time and money in the long run.

As you come to step 4, tactical planning, it is here you are assigning responsibilities for execution and action; you are forming teams and delegating responsibilities. This action will bring your strategic thinking and planning to life. This is at the 70 to 80 percent stage of your process. You are beginning to let go, but you still need some confirmation of your strategy. You need real situations to prove your theories, so don't wait to be perfect. After all, as a leader, you are already thinking about what's next, right?

In each step of this process, you must be communicating to your organization. Change is scary, and left unexplained, change will be defined by anyone who speaks up. It is best that the definition of why change is happening, what the change is, when the change will happen, how the change will affect me, and how we will be better off after the change has happened comes from leadership, the people that know about the change and are causing it to happen. People want to know as much about the facts of a change situation as can be related. If they are not given the facts in a timely manner, they will come up with their own answers, and often times, their made up answers take people in a different direction.

The change communication must be frequent and confident. It must have enough information to satisfy the concerned yet not too much so as you are not tied to perceived commitments. You need flexibility to adjust as your process reveals itself during your full implementation process. You want to have your people informed and excited about what is coming, not scared to move forward. You want them engaged, to offer their best thinking and best effort.

As an aside, you are also trying to define those people who will not support your future vision, whether they are on the fence or they are vocal dissenters. You will never get 100 percent of your organization to support any major change, but if you follow the 20-70-10 rule, 20 percent of the people will get on board quickly, 70 percent will need to be shown the value, the proof, the "what's in it for me," and the 10 percent who will never support the plan. You want to focus on the 90 percent of your organization whom you can move forward. The 10 percent will help you to weed them out because they don't want to put forth the effort to change.

A strategic planning process is about looking to the future. It is a deliberate process with deliberate expectations. Take your time; don't rush it. Use the resources at your disposal and those that reveal themselves along the journey, and don't forget to let people know what you're doing and, most importantly, why.

POINT 8— INDUSTRY LEADER
AS A LEADER...

Point 8: Understand what it means to work for a recognized leader in an industry, and all the responsibilities and frustrations that distinction brings.

Recognition is an interesting thing; everyone wants it until they don't. When you think about recognition, what comes first to your mind, positive recognition or negative recognition? Heck, I'll bet you were only thinking about positive recognition until you read the word "negative." Recognition comes in many forms—positive, negative, non, and all the variations therein, and it comes from many different sources. It is how you manage your recognition, both sought and unsought, that counts as a leader. It is how you manage your reaction and responsibility as a leader that matters more than you may realize, and yes, it can be frustrating, because you can't control all recognition.

As a leader in an organization, by default, you represent the organization in all that it stands for, whether you like it or not. By simply saying, "I work for _____," you take on all the characteristics of that organization in a person's mind. It really doesn't matter if you agree or disagree with a company position on anything, by default, you *are* the company, and at times, things can get very interesting. In today's world of social media, in an instant, your words and actions and those of your organization can be heard and seen by others all over the world, and you can't control the reaction to how the communication is received. Now that's recognition!

So how do you gain some element of control over the types of recognition you can control for your organization? What can you do as a leader to influence more positive recognition and blunt the unwarranted or misunderstood negative recognition that will occur in today's ever more connected world? A first step is to understand how *you* are viewed as a leader.

- What do others say about your influence ability, your organization knowledge, your organization credibility?
- Are you confident in your message delivery?
- Are you consistent with your message remarks?
- Do you say the right things to the right audiences at the right times?
- Do you deliver messages in good times and bad?
- Are you respected for your messages?
- Are your responses positive, negative, or neutral?
- What are you doing to enhance your reputation with those you can influence so you can have greater influence in your ability to message for yourself and on behalf of your organization?

No one will do it for you; you must do it for yourself.

One very important element you must understand as a leader when it comes to recognition is that you can't control all the recognition either you or your organization will receive. However, you can influence the frequency and content of what you want to be out in the open, but it will be far less than 100 percent control of all the recognition that will occur. You must accept that fact and work on that which you can influence in the direction you want things to go. It may be frustrating, but it is reality, and you must accept it.

But you say, "I don't work for an industry leader." Oh, so you think recognition doesn't matter? The image you portray as a leader and an organization doesn't matter? If I may be candid, it does matter, and let me relate how it matters.

You have people who rely on you—your family, your subordinates, your coworkers, and those who rely on your organization to provide what you offer. You and your organization mean something to many people. Now think if they didn't like you or didn't want to do business with your organization. They would leave you as an employer, your customers would find someone else to provide the services you offer, and your family, well, I'll leave that for you to figure out and work through.

Working for any kind of organization, big or small, local or national, domestic or international, has its own set of challenges when it comes to how it wants to be known or recognized within the industry in which it does business. As the leader or a leader within the organization, you have responsibilities to promote your organization. It is in how you promote your organization and how you influence others to promote your organization that will lessen or increase the challenges your organization faces or how you will draw others—potential employees, customers, clients, donors, advocates—to your organization to sing its praises to those you can't reach directly.

POINT 9—EGOS
AS A LEADER...

> Point 9: Learn how to work with and deal with egos, starting with your own. This is not just for you, but coach others to do the same.

"Wow I'm good!" Don't you get up every morning and make that statement when you look at yourself in the mirror? After all, if you don't believe in yourself, how can you get others to believe in you and follow you as a leader? You have to be good. People have to know you are good; people have to believe in you so *you* will continue to be successful. And what about others—as long as you are doing well, as long as you feel good about what you are doing, as long as you are being recognized for your success as a leader, do others matter? As Muhammad Ali exclaimed, "I am the greatest!"

Your ego, isn't it wonderful? Belief in yourself and your abilities is a foundational element of success in leadership or any other kind of success. However, if I may offer, it is how you demonstrate your self-confidence in your actions and words that will either draw people to you as a leader or repel them to seek other leadership. Understanding how your ego evolves and how you can change it is an enlightening journey.

As I was growing up, I had early failures in my social experiences, but they were unknown to me at the time. I was a very active child. My attention span was pretty short. I knew what was going on, but if it didn't interest me long enough to hold my attention, I went on to something else. I was impatient. These early missteps had compounding implications as I continued my education through elementary, middle, and high school. I was happy to be an underachieving C student in high school who did enough to get by. I was more of a follower than a leader. But I had people who didn't want to let me be satisfied with my chosen path in life of underachieving, people who kept pushing me and pushing me and pushing me until I finally started to listen.

My leadership light was turned on the summer after I graduated from high school. I didn't want to go to college. To be honest, my grades didn't qualify me for many colleges. My parents helped me with an alternate route, one that led to a trade school to learn the profession of aviation support. It was during this away-from-home, three-month experience that I found, when I applied myself, I was actually pretty smart. I found that other students would look to me asking for guidance and understanding with their course work. The information I provided to them helped with their understanding of the content, and they did well. I graduated with a 95 percent average, which is not bad for a C student. It was a revealing experience.

After spending that fall and the spring of the following year looking for a job and pumping gas in Georgetown (Washington, DC), I came to the conclusion that I did not want to pump gas the rest of my life and indeed did want to go on to college. For the fall of 1972, I was accepted to a small college in Jamestown, North Dakota. It was there that my confidence, dare I say my ego, took off. I was a solid B student in college. I was involved in varsity athletics and did very well. I was involved in student leadership and the college newspaper. I was well known on campus, and I easily thought, *Man, I'm good!* My ego boomed, and I was not shy about exclaiming my confidence in my intellectual or physical abilities.

Upon graduation, my confidence continued to gain altitude. Of seventeen job interviews, I had fourteen offers, selecting a position with a large retailer as an executive trainee. Once I started my career, I very confidently demonstrated success and was moved along the success track. I wanted more and kept telling people how good I was both personally and professionally. In hindsight, this was the beginning of a major professional learning, a negative one, and one that I have tried to help others not experience.

Think of those you work with, those people who tell you how smart they are, how well others think of them, about their latest success or idea, how good they will do with this or that, that someday they will be _____. I'm confident you know some people like this. There is a very fine line between confidence and conceit. Unfortunately, early in my career, I found myself to be more perceived in the latter grouping.

In my quest to help others not make the mistakes of my earlier underachieving, I found I was thrusting my opinions and actions on others. I was becoming known as a know it all because I always had an answer and shared it unrequested with those I perceived to be in need of an answer. I started noticing people not wanting to engage with me and sensed something was wrong.

I then started watching those leaders I admired and took note of their actions, words, and tone. I learned to look for what defines a confident leader. I found the following:

- Confident leaders are capable of backing up their words with the right actions that engage and encourage others to achieve their own success, whatever their success may be.

- Confident leaders demonstrate their leadership; they don't have to tell you about it.

- Confident leaders continually learn from the mistakes of their past, and they observe the mistakes of others and try not to repeat those same types of errors.

- Confident leaders encourage others. They listen; they don't tell.

- Confident leaders allow difference of opinion to occur because everyone can learn from a different perspective. You can learn to embrace the difference or you can learn that you chose not to, but you learn when a leader provides the environment for the learning to take place.

Your ego is something that you control. If you are happy with the way things are and you are not distancing those you work with or seeing them not seek you out, then I would offer you are doing fairly well. However, I would offer you can always do better as a leader. All you have to do is listen to what others say or don't say about your leadership. The answers are all around you as a leader, and there are people willing to let you know if all you do is ask the question, as awkward as it may feel.

An effective and inclusive leader checks their ego against others. There really is nothing they need to prove other than delivering on or exceeding the expectations of their position. They work with and encourage others to excel at their position. They offer guidance; they don't force their insights on others. If their offer of guidance is not accepted, no big deal; the world will keep on spinning, and they can move on to engaging others in their journey of success. Be the leader others admire.

POINT 10—DON'T THROW MONEY AT THINGS

AS A LEADER...

> Point 10: Don't throw money at things as solutions.
> Be penny wise, not pound (dollar) foolish.

The bottom line, the bottom line; be mindful of the bottom line. Reinvesting in the business is something all keen leaders do, when they have the money to do so. Prudently targeting funding for future-oriented projects is a necessary part of organization growth. Just like you would do for your family, setting aside money for a rainy day, or better yet for retirement, is something smart people do. You can't just fly by the seat of your pants as a leader leading a project team or an organization. You must have a concept of what you are doing, why you are doing it, what you will get out of it, and the resources needed to achieve the goals from a financial perspective.

"Dad, can I have $20?"

"For what?"

"Just because." Did you ever have a conversation like that in your house?

"Just give me more funding, and I'll get it done." Sound like a question posed to you at work?

You can't just throw money at things. Well, you can, but you shouldn't if you don't have it or you need it for other things. When your child says "just because" as reasoning for asking for money, do you just give them the money or do you want to know why they need the money? My experience is that I want to know why they want the money and what they plan to do with it. Call me overprotective or maybe even cheap, but I want to know where my money is going and how it will be used.

As a leader, you sometimes function as a bank. People come to you requesting funds for things. You have to make decisions based on a number of factors, including, but not limited to, do you have the funds, what are the funds going to be used for, is the request within the scope of your responsibilities, will the funds be put to good use, and will the funds help the organization grow? You must protect the organizations' assets. You are responsible for the portion of the assets within your control.

Would you lay a pile of money out in the open and let everyone know they can take what they want and do with it as they please, first come, first served? I seriously doubt it. As someone responsible for assets of an organization, you have a basic expectation of a return on your investment. If you work for a publicly traded company, you have a fiduciary responsibility to ensure company assets are used properly, and your shareholders *do* expect a return on their investment, and they don't want to see money wasted.

As a leader, you must understand how funding requests will be used. You simply can't just give away money. You can't.

People that expect you can or you should probably aren't the people you should have working for you. They need to come to you with justification, good justification, on why they need the funding, what they will do with the funding, the anticipated results (ROI, return on investment), and any possible alternatives. If you do not receive this information without asking, then you have some work to do as a leader in setting expectations on how to obtain funding. After all, you don't have an open checkbook or unlimited funds. You don't just throw money at things now do you? Good leaders don't!

However, and there is usually a however with money, I'm sure you have discretionary funds that you can do with as you please, right? This discretionary funding is your cushion for those unforeseen events that come up that require funding that was not defined or anticipated during your budgeting process or to take advantage of an opportunity that surfaces during the budget cycle. These opportunities happen and, in some cases, are necessary to take advantage of to keep moving forward and stay relevant.

I would challenge that you still do not blindly throw money at something without a reasonable explanation on need, use, and results. Smart leaders have money cushions or know where these cushions exist and how to access them. Smart leaders plan ahead and keep funding reserves. Smart leaders let their subordinates know about the budgeting process and expectations of expenditures against the budget and that everyone, including the leader, is accountable for delivering expected results in their own right on the funding that is provided to them.

POINT 11—
SEEK UNDERSTANDING
AS A LEADER...

> Point 11: You must seek understanding from your
> boss, your peers, your subordinates, and your clients,
> not the other way around.

A leader must have a vision, an idea of where they want to lead others. However, the journey is not something a leader can undertake alone. The leader must have support and encouragement to move along the path of their journey, and that support can come in many forms.

- Will your vision be supported by those above you?

- Will your vision be supported by those in similar leadership roles?

- Will your vision be supported by those who will carry out the details of the work?

- Will your vision be supported by those who will hopefully desire your offering?

The answer to each of these questions is in how much you understand about each of these groups and how they might be attracted to your vision or from a learning perspective, not attracted to your vision. Each of these groups can be a supporter of your vision or a detractor to your vision. Identifying those who would and will devalue your vision early and then adjusting your vision or their understanding is critical to your forward momentum. In parallel, identifying those who will advocate for your vision at the outset increases your ability to remain focused on the strategic elements of your vision while still having your voice heard within the groups.

Each group is unique, and each group is important to the success of your vision. In your mind, your vision can be the greatest thing since _____, but if there is no one who will purchase your vision, you will go nowhere. A leader dramatically increases where they can grow personally and professionally when they have multiple support bases for their vision and they have an understanding of the needs of all those around them.

Now you may be thinking, *If I want someone to understand something, I will tell them what to understand.* Ah, a sign of frustration and arcane leadership. In today's more expansive work environments where there are many more choices as to where, with whom, and even how to work, a leader must continually take the time to understand all those with whom they interact. It does take time. It does take patience. It can and most likely will be frustrating, but the long-term payoff will benefit many.

Hold face-to-face meetings with different groups, and I mean different groups—generational, tenure, geography, ethnicity, nationality, position, etcetera—to gain deep insight into their understanding of your direction and sometimes, even you as a leader. Do this continually and not just in times of crisis, especially not just in times of crisis. Seeking understanding in good times and bad helps reassure you and those who rely on you that you have a grasp on what is needed to keep moving forward.

Now you may be thinking, *It's great to hold these meetings, but how do I get people to tell me what they really think?* Let me offer you a process that has served me well in a number of different discovery situations, personal and professional, to bring forth perspectives in diverse groups. It is called Stop, Start, Continue. I'll bet you might have heard of this process that had its origins in organizational change discovery. Here's how I have used this process with success.

THE SETUP

1. An invitation goes to a group, three to thirty, of similarly situated people—that is, a team, peers, clients, etcetera—asking them to attend a discovery meeting.

2. I work to define a framing question that the group can focus on that will help surface issues and opportunities to success.

3. I let all participants know that we are here to discover information on how we can be more efficient and effective in our roles to achieve XXX. As an example, I have used this process to gain insight on me as a

leader, and I used this same process with my children as their father. "As your father, what is one thing you would want me to stop, start, continue?" or "As your boss, what is one thing you would want me to stop, start, continue?" Each exercise brought forth very illuminating results that allowed me to take action.

4. I give each participant a pad of 3×5 Post-it notes. I have found that having group participants use Post-it notes to write down their answers ensures everyone becomes engaged.

5. On the side, I have three pre-prepared areas or easels with the separate headings of "Stop," "Start," "Continue."

THE PROCESS

1. When everyone is situated, I reveal the framing question and why it was chosen. I further relate I would like everyone's candid perspective in answering the question.

2. I then explain the exercise I will be taking everyone through and that I call it the "one thing" exercise. Each participant is asked to write down "one thing" on one Post-it note that they feel I, we, or the organization (depends on what you are going after) should stop, start, and continue. They can complete as many

"one thing" notes for each of stop, start, or continue but only have one comment per Post-it note.

3. I also let everyone know that I will be breaking the group up into smaller groups to look at all the responses and that what goes up does not guarantee that action will be taken but that it will at least be discussed for understanding.

4. When everyone is done, I ask the participants to post their notes under the respective "Stop," "Start," "Continue" heading and retake their seats.

5. Next I have them count off by threes and assign the 1s to "Stop," the 2s to "Start," and the 3s to "Continue."

6. Each group is then tasked with culling down their group of Post-it notes to three to five topical items.

7. When all is done, a report out is done by each group.

THE CONCLUSION

1. By having everyone write down their responses, you eliminate a person or two dominating the discussion in an open capture exercise and enable the participation of everyone in the group.

2. Stop is usually defined as those items the group does not value.

3.   Start is usually defined as those items or actions that are currently not being done, that the group would like to do or be done.

4.   Continue is usually defined as those items the group values.

5.   The follow-through action is left to the leader.

This exercise is very good at being inclusive from an understanding perspective and does generate accountabilities for the leader from a follow-through aspect and maybe even action items that have broader impact that can be assigned to group members. It works; try it for greater and broader understanding!

POINT 12—PATIENCE AND PERSISTENCE

AS A LEADER...

Point 12: Patience and persistence are valuable virtues.

Drip, drip, drip, drip, drip, drip, drip. A continual single drip of water on a rock, over time—yes, lots of time—will change the face of a rock. Following that same analogy, yet in a much more modern context, will have the same effect on organization efforts. "There is a time and place for everything"—ever heard of that idiom? I'm sure you have; however, I would offer that you most likely heard it from someone who was telling you no on some request or action you were seeking.

An inclusive leader has a timing patience, an instinct if you will, that tells them when to push and when to hold back. They subtly yet continually test their ideas with different groups to determine if the timing is right to push their idea further for broader acceptance. Notice I say "Test their ideas with different groups." By testing, by running different trials, insight will be gained for adjustments that may be needed for acceptance within that particular group, and there may be benefits to other groups that had not been considered.

An inclusive leader should not be so myopic that they focus on only one idea or concept as they move along their journey or that they receive validation from only one group.

They must be flexible, and they must also be persistent. It is the continual efforts made by leaders yet not efforts that are defined as "There he goes again" that will win interest and eventual support from the broadest audience. I have been known to call it a special patience and drive for success.

"Wait for it...wait for it...wait for it...now go!" As a professional, no matter what your profession is, we have the inherent belief that opportunities will come and opportunities will reveal themselves. It is a special patience that evolves in a leader to wait for it that is developed over time via trial and error. You learn via your mistakes, or your missteps, that maybe if you had waited just a bit longer to move on your idea, the drive, you could have achieved your desire. Sometimes you learn that you must seize the moment and go for it to take advantage of something. You learn from your mistakes. I offer in either case, it does take a special patience to learn about timing and then the additional learning about the "go for it" or drive to achieve your goal.

Remember when you really wanted something when you were younger at home? You would think about the timing if you asked either your mother or your father. You learned over time, through trial and error, that if someone was not in a good mood, it was not a good time to ask for something because you would most likely be responded to with a very quick no! You learned patience, you learned timing, you learned approach tactics...because your goal was a yes.

I would also offer that it was during your youth that you also learned persistence. If you wanted something and you wanted it bad enough, no matter how many no's you received, you just kept asking. However, after each no answer, you modified your ask from a timing standpoint; you might even have modified your ask from a content standpoint, and when your skills were really sharp, you might even have had someone else do your ask, but the key is that you were persistent in your asking to get to that ultimate yes.

The lessons and learning of our youth continually reveal themselves during our lifetime. Those lessons were built on a foundation of patience and persistence.

POINT 13—ANTICIPATE
AS A LEADER...

> Point 13: Anticipate...business, people, clients, suppliers, community, yourself, and the X factor.

One of my very favorite words, "anticipate"—in my thinking, the art of predicting the future. I say art versus science from the perspective that so many things go into predicting future outcomes—such as action and reaction—to the decisions that are made and then the counter decisions made based on the prior decision and so forth to get to the desired result. Nothing is perfect in any decision process, but the better a leader is at anticipating what *may* happen and then planning for what they *may* do in response, the better chance they are at being successful in the event *it* happens.

In the seventh grade, during my homeroom time, I learned to play chess. A few of us who were challenged academically started to play the game. We found chess to be mentally stimulating, as there were so many different moves that could be taken to checkmate the king. As we played more, we continued to be intrigued because the game made us think. I had to anticipate my opponents move and plan my next move based on their reaction to my move. To be good, I had to anticipate two or three moves ahead; it was intriguing and fun. In checkmating the king, how I did it, how long it took, how many pieces I would lose along the way would only be shown as I played out the game. I tried to anticipate each of my moves and my opponent's reaction to my moves, but invariably, there were surprises, something I did not plan for, a move I did not anticipate. Many times I was met with an "I did not think my opponent would make that move" in an expected manner or risks I was willing to take such as piece sacrifices so I could move closer to capturing the king didn't happen like I had planned.

It was during these games that I learned the basics of strategic planning. At the beginning of each game, I planned out my first three moves. Based on my opponent's response to my moves, I either stayed on plan or began to alter my plan. As underachieving seventh graders who did not find interest in academics, we found the experimentation and learning that occurred during the game of chess to be stimulating, challenging, and ultimately fun. Some members of the group took to reading deeper about chess and different strategies and tactics on moves, and we shared our learning.

I remember the day I mastered the four-move checkmate. It was great when it worked, but it only worked for a short time on the novice members of our small group. Once someone learns your moves, they learn how to counter them to blunt your attack so they can gain the advantage. These were lessons that would come to bear later in my life, but all came down to the one word, "anticipate."

In many of the facilitations I have done on strategic planning, early in the session I invariably will ask two questions:

(1) Does anyone have a really good crystal ball to predict the future? (2) Can anyone read minds really well? The answer to both of these questions is met with silence to which I state, "Then we must dialogue, discuss, challenge, anticipate, and plan the future we want to create together." To a degree, I'm stating the obvious, but it never ceases to amaze me how many people think someone knows *all* the answers. No one person has all the answers. The answer may be in the collective body of people gathered to create the plan, but everyone must open up and provide their best thinking and experience, understanding that no one person knows all.

Now apply the chess metaphor—anticipating moves—to your organization, to your employees, to your clients, to those that supply your organization resources, to the communities in which you do business, to yourself, and to the unknown.

- Can you plan for every contingency?
- Can you anticipate every possible interaction?
- Can you plan for feelings?
- Can you plan for those things that are not within your control?

The short answer is obviously no to all these questions, but you can do one thing, and that is plan. Without a response plan to anything, to any move, why play the game?

Effective planning is a key element for every person and a critical competency for every leader. We all plan. We all try to guess what the near and far future will hold; we all anticipate that future. It is those people, those leaders, that build around their anticipation with actionable elements that come to life, who will lead themselves and others to the future they want to create as they all move along the path of their success.

POINT 14—CREDIBILITY
AS A LEADER...

> Point 14: Understand the fragility of credibility, personally and as a business.

"You are as good as your word." Remember when a person's word was their bond? Some of you might, but unfortunately for many others, they have never known a time when a person's promise or commitment makes a huge statement as to who they are as a person. Personally, when I or someone else makes a commitment, I expect the commitment to be upheld. If it can't, there needs to be a very good reason, and then I would expect to apologize personally or be apologized to for not being able to uphold my commitment. This lesson was taught to me by my parents. *My how times have changed.*

There's another quote I also like that pertains to credibility, "Fool me once, shame on you; fool me twice, shame on me." I'll give most people a benefit of the doubt. However, when the doubt becomes a pattern, I can no longer trust a person, and they have lost their credibility with me. I will no longer go to them or use them or buy from them.

A leader has many responsibilities. I would offer that their first responsibility is to themselves. They must make a commitment to be trustworthy, honest, moral, and ethical to the person they see in the mirror. I don't mean it to sound like you have to take the Boy Scout's Oath or the Girl Scout's

Promise, but if you are not honest with yourself, how can you be honest and credible with others? Credibility starts with the individual (yourself).

Credibility may start with the individual, but it continues to grow with and through others, and it is only maintained by others and not the individual. I could tell you how credible, honest, and trustworthy I am, but if you don't see it, if you don't believe it, then I am not credible in your eyes. There is something I do or have done that tarnishes my credibility, and I must seek to understand what I did to be less than credible. I must then work to fix the issue. I will only know I have regained my credibility when I hear or see from others that I have done so.

I really don't know if this ever happened, but there's a story of the bridge builder. He built one hundred bridges. One of them collapsed. Which one is his credibility tied to? Yep, the one that collapsed. His credibility in 99 percent of the other bridges, the ones still standing, is totally offset by the 1 percent of his bridges that failed. Does this impact his bridge-building business? Most certainly it does, and he has to work extremely hard to regain or reestablish the credibility, value, and safety of his bridges, if he ever can.

Think of yourself and your organization. How do you project your credibility as a leader and reflect the credibility of your organization? Is the projection and reflection different, similar, or the same? As a leader, can you separate yourself from your organization with regard to credibility?

Credibility is very internal. It is part of who you are as a person and what your organization is as an entity. Credibility evolves over time, and there is no time limit. You build your personal credibility, as your organization builds its credibility, over time. There is interdependency between you as the leader and the organization you represent. You want people to continue to follow you as a leader, and your organization wants people to keep coming back for repeat business. If you both are credible, if you both are genuine, you both will grow.

POINT 15—UNDERSTAND
AS A LEADER...

Point 15: Understand:

- You have the opportunity to contribute on a global scale, no matter how small things may appear.
- You have an unspoken influence over hundreds of thousands of people, if not millions.
- The financial orientation of your organization and be mindful of its bottom line.
- Your future is yours to make...or break.

So it all comes down to this last point, number 15, but with four subpoints. You are a leader. You want to grow. You want to help others grow. You want your organization to grow. There are just a few more things you should understand and consider to be a more inclusive leader:

1. The world is shrinking, not physically, but in how we communicate, how we do business, where our employees come from, and where we secure our organizational resources. Almost any organization contributes in some small way to the global economy. When you break everything down—from where you buy your products, to who owns your property, to the languages that are spoken in your organization—I

would be very willing to wager a small sum of money, you will be very surprised at the reach of your organization, no matter how small or large you may be.

2. As you consider the reach of your organization, does your reach go beyond the visible walls of your organization? The answer is most certainly yes. With the expansiveness of technology and with the creativity and use of social media, your ability to become visible and create impressions with a global audience has never been so easy. Done with intent, in a purposeful manner, your impressions can literally change the world. You must understand the ability and opportunity that is within your reach.

3. No matter your functional expertise, you must understand organizational finance. Where does the money come from and go to? Do you understand the difference between donations, revenue, and sales and what they mean, if applicable to your organization? What does the "bottom line" mean in your organization? When all is said and done, you can't spend more than you bring in if you want to remain viable. As a leader, you must understand the finances.

4. The future is yours. It is what you make of it. You have no one else who can or will make it for you. It is all up to you. No one, especially a leader, can abdicate their own future. You are the one, the only one who will craft what you will become.

WHAT'S NEXT?

PAYING IT FORWARD

My dream sequence…

1. Think your dream.
2. Believe in your dream.
3. Develop your dream.
4. Speak your dream.
5. Realize your dream.

From a remedial reader to a person who *helps people do things they don't think they can do* to a corporate spokesperson and now to an author, I'm realizing my dream, dreams I didn't even realize I had until they revealed themselves over time with the help of many others.

What's your dream? What's holding you back? If you don't think it, believe in it, develop it, and finally speak it, well you know the conclusion. Only you can make it happen!

Go impress the person you see in the mirror so *that* person can help others.

Be a leader, and be blessed!

JUST FOR FUN, SERIOUSLY...DENNISISMS TO MAKE YOU THINK

1. *Change people or change people.* As a Leader, you must change people to contributors, or you must change people to contribute somewhere else.

2. *Take care of your people, and they'll take care of you. Don't take care of your people, and they'll still take care of you!* As a leader, taking care of your people should be a priority so they feel valued and add to the success of themselves, the organization, and you. Don't take care of your people, and see what happens. I don't think I need to tell you.

3. *If you want something and never ask the question, the answer will always be no.* As a leader, if you want something, give yourself half a chance to get it by at least asking for it. If you don't ask for it, there's a 100 percent chance you won't get it.

4. *See with your ears. Hear with your eyes.* As a leader, you must use all your senses to your advantage. However,

you don't have to use them as intended. After all, I think my mother had eyes in the back of her head!

5. *If yesterday you said, "I'll do it tomorrow," you might as well do it today.* As a leader, get things done. Don't put them off until tomorrow; do them today!

6. *People are myopic.* As a leader, don't let a person's narrow view of a situation blur your vision of where you need to go.

7. *Have aspirational foresight with validated hindsight.* As a leader, learn from your past mistakes, but don't let them hold you back from where you want to go.

8. *It's never been done is not a reason for not doing it.* As a leader, create your way of doing something that has never been done for the greater good.

9. *Don't recruit anyone to work for you; attract them.* As a leader, if you have to talk people into working for you (recruiting), then you haven't done enough yet to make people want to work for you (attraction).

10. *There's more to see than what we see.* As a leader, look beyond the surface of what you see in a person. How we appear, how we think, how we act is an amalgamation of such difference that you must dig below the surface to find the true value in the person.